MANIFEST YOUR MILLIONS!

A Lottery Winner Shares His Law of Attraction Secrets

WRITTEN BY

EDDIE CORONADO

Copyright 2013

All Rights Reserved

The cover image was taken during my appearance on the California Lottery television broadcast of The Big Spin. Several million tickets were entered but only a small handful of finalists were invited to the show. I took home $50,000.00 that day!

A year later I won another lottery jackpot of $193,600.00!

...all through The Law of Attraction!

Let me teach you how the Law of Attraction really works!

WHY YOU NEED TO READ THIS BOOK

This is one of the most powerful Law of Attraction books you will ever read. It was written by a lottery winner who understands how the Law of Attraction works and how it can be used to attract money. The Law of Attraction is not a fly-by-night fad, but a powerfully creative force that can give you the life of your dreams if you know how to use it, so the better you understand this power the faster it will manifest your desires. By reading this book you will learn proven strategies that will help you manifest money, a new job, a life partner, a lucrative business or anything else that you can make a part of your beliefs and feelings. Everyday millions of people are introduced to the Law of Attraction through books, CDs and other materials. Unfortunately, only a small percentage of these people achieve their goals because much of this information fails to present an accurate explanation of this power and how to use it effectively, but this book will give hope to millions of people who want to learn the secrets of the Law of Attraction. While writing this book it was my intention that you learn about the Law of Attraction without having to read through hundreds of pages of boring filler, so I created a book that explains the facts quickly and clearly so that you can begin manifesting money as soon as you understand the concepts presented in this book.

WHAT MAKES THIS BOOK SO UNIQUE?

This book contains a number of unique perspectives that are proven to work. After explaining what the Law of Attraction is and how it responds to intention, I discuss the power of Affirmations and how to use them effectively. Next is a section on Creative Visualization that contains two parts. Part one explains the history of creative visualization and the quantum effects it has on the world around us. Part two deals with the Four Essential Elements of creative visualization and explains how this faculty can be used effectively. The following chapter on Gratitude and Receiving provides powerful tools to help you attract whatever you set your intention on. One chapter that I am particularly fond of is called Living in Balance, which is the most important chapter of this book. The metaphysical ideas explained in this chapter are so profound that this information must be understood and implemented in order to make the Law of Attraction work. No amount of affirmations and creative visualizations will work unless you understand the spiritual importance of Living in Balance. I have also included a Question-and-Answer section in which I respond to many of the most important Law of Attraction questions that people have asked me. Finally, this book concludes with a chapter detailing my Prosperity Action Plan, which is the plan I implemented and followed to manifest lottery prizes and other wonderful things in my life.

INTRODUCTION

I wrote this book because I wanted to share my insights on the Law of Attraction. Having successfully used this power, I felt that my contribution was necessary because so many people misunderstand this spiritual law and its use. It is my desire that readers throughout the world make the quantum leap from knowing about this power to using it effectively. Manifestation through the Law of Attraction is not a privilege set aside for certain people. The Law of Attraction can be used by the housewife, the single man, the businesswoman, the policeman, the minister, or the young person in school. This awesome power is an inherent part of every human being, and can be used by you to the same degree that it has been used by anyone else on the planet. So as you read my book keep in mind that there is no limit to the success you can experience through the Law of Attraction. If you believe that you will win the lottery, then so be it! If you believe that you can have the car, job and life of your dreams with lots of money to enjoy, then you can manifest those things, too! My success in winning lottery prizes will prove far more convincing than all the books that can be written about this subject. I am convinced that through my book you will understand how the Law of Attraction works and will use it to manifest the desires of your heart.

TABLE OF CONTENTS

WHY YOU NEED TO READ THIS BOOK 4

WHAT MAKES THIS BOOK SO UNIQUE? 6

INTRODUCTION 8

CHAPTER 1: WHAT IS THE LAW OF ATTRACTION? 11

CHAPTER 2: THE PROSPERING POWER OF AFFIRMATIONS 23

CHAPTER 3: CREATIVE VISUALIZATION, PART 1 33

CHAPTER 4: CREATIVE VISUALIZATION, PART 2 49

CHAPTER 5: GRATITUDE AND RECEIVING 56

CHAPTER 6: LIVING IN BALANCE 68

CHAPTER 7: QUESTIONS AND ANSWERS ABOUT THE UNIVERSAL LAW 77

CHAPTER 8: THE PROSPERITY ACTION PLAN 98

CHAPTER 1

WHAT IS THE LAW OF ATTRACTION?

The Law of Attraction is an infinite spiritual technology that is available to everyone. It can be used by any person willing to learn about its characteristics and then follow a particular set of guidelines until the end result is accomplished. This is possible because the Law of Attraction is a reliable force that is set in motion through the power of human thoughts. We refer to this spiritual technology as a law because it is repeatable like the law of gravity, which is repeatable under specific conditions. According to the dictionary, a law is a statement or a fact in which a natural or scientific phenomenon always occurs if certain conditions are present. The Law of

Attraction, or Universal Law, is a spiritual certainty because it can be demonstrated over and over as long as certain mental and emotional conditions are met.

We have at our command the most powerful tool known to mankind, our mind. Most of us, unfortunately, have never been taught how to use it effectively. Moreover, millions of people have accepted the belief that they must settle for the ordinary even though they have an extraordinary potential within themselves that can just as easily create massive success and abundance. The power within our minds can heal us, prosper us, attract ideal circumstances, and even materialize the perfect job or life partner. The same power that keeps us stuck in poverty and limitation can prosper us and give us the life of our dreams if we understand how to speak its language. Psychologists say that we are only using about 10% of our brain power, and some reliable sources claim that we actually use much less than that. Whatever the percentage, humanity is awakening to an awareness in which we are finally recognizing the creative power of our thoughts and feelings. The Twenty First Century is considered by mystics as a major turning point of human evolution. It is the dawning of the Age of Aquarius in its broadest sense, an era in which human evolution takes a giant leap into greater awareness and personal power.

This awareness demonstrates that humans are not merely a collection of tissues and bones, but dynamic, spiritual beings that are more intricately connected to the Universe than was imagined when our ancestors first gazed into the heavens to ponder the origins of life. Until the Twentieth Century, mankind and the universe were considered two separate entities completely unrelated to one another in terms of their physical makeup and function, but enlightened scientists and quantum physicists have shown us that humanity and the universe are intricately related on a subatomic, or quantum, level in a manner suggesting that everything in existence is a result of consciousness being aware of itself and the things around it.

The following quotes are attributed to a number of respected scientists throughout the world who have discovered that consciousness ultimately influences events in the physical world.

These people comprise a growing community of enlightened thinkers who have agreed on one basic idea: THOUGHTS BECOME THINGS.

"Atoms or elementary particles themselves are not real; they form a world of potentialities or possibilities rather than one of things or facts." — Nobel Prize winner, Werner Heisenberg, German theoretical physicist and one of the key creators of quantum mechanics.

"Anyone not shocked by quantum mechanics has not yet understood it." — Nobel Prize winner, Niels Bohr, Danish physicist who made foundational contributions to understanding atomic structure and quantum mechanics.

"Everything we call real is made of things that cannot be regarded as real." — Niels Bohr

"I regard consciousness as fundamental. I regard matter as derivative from consciousness. We cannot get behind consciousness. Everything that we talk about, everything that we regard as existing, postulates consciousness." — Nobel Prize winner, Max Planck, German theoretical physicist who originated quantum theory.

"As a man who has devoted his whole life to the most clear headed science, to the study of matter, I can tell you as a result of my research about atoms this much: There is no matter as such. All matter originates and exists only by virtue of a force which brings the particle of an atom to vibration and holds this most minute solar system of the atom together. We must assume behind this force the existence of a conscious and intelligent mind." — Max Planck

"Observations not only disturb what is to be measured, they produce it." – Pascual Jordan, theoretical/mathematical physicist who made significant contributions to quantum mechanics and quantum field theory.

"The doctrine that the world is made up of objects whose existence is independent of human consciousness turns out to be in conflict with quantum mechanics and with facts established by experiment." – Bernard d'Espagnat, French theoretical physicist, philosopher of science and author best known for his work on the nature of reality.

"The universe exists because we are aware of it." — Martin Rees, British cosmologist and astrophysicist

"Our thought processes are much more intimately connected to the physical world than any of us would suspect." — Dr. David Peat, physicist and author of The Bridge Between Matter and Mind

Prior to the birth of quantum physics a number of mystics and spiritual teachers shared similar opinions about the nature of reality, which is that the physical world is much less physical than previously thought. Ministers, New Thought practitioners, philosophers, Tibetan monks, and visionaries like Thomas Troward and Joseph Murphy, understood that a change in consciousness would result in a change in physical conditions. It was during the mid-Twentieth Century that quantum physics and spirituality met with agreement that human consciousness is creative. Prior to that, many unexplainable events were considered miracles because early observers did not understand the mechanics of quantum physics and the ways in which the Universal Law responded to thoughts and feelings.

Long before the Law of Attraction was a household phrase, New Thought pioneer Prentice Mulford wrote a book titled Thoughts Are Things, in which he explained that the things we talk about and think about eventually become our experience. A short time later Ernest Holmes, founder of the Church of Religious Science, taught his parishioners that life is a mirror that will reflect to the thinker what he thinks into it. As the interest in Mental Science grew, books such as The Magic of Believing by Claude Bristol and The Power of Awareness by Neville Goddard became so popular that publishers worked overtime to keep them on the shelves. These best sellers were followed by books, tapes and CDs by teachers such as Wayne Dyer, Louise Hay, Stuart Wilde and Bob Proctor teaching that we can positively influence events and circumstances in our lives once we have learned to use both parts of our minds effectively.

We all have one mind that contains two distinct characteristics. These two characteristics are known as the conscious mind and the subconscious mind. These aspects of our minds have been thoroughly studied and are well-established facts within the world of psychology. In fact, some of the most influential psychologists in the world have written about the duality of human consciousness. William James, known as the father of American psychology, understood the transformational power of both sides of the mind, yet he noted the significance of the subconscious mind when he wrote, "The power to move the world is in your subconscious mind." Therefore, let us take a brief look at the two distinct aspects of the human mind before we look at how to manifest money with this awesome power.

- The Conscious mind consists of everything that is within our conscious awareness, which includes thoughts, feelings, memories, sensations and perceptions that exist within our current awareness. The conscious mind is personal and selective, meaning that it has the ability to choose what it wants to do and what it wants to focus on. The very fact that the conscious mind possesses the ability to choose means that it can turn from one course of action to another with a single thought. The power of the conscious mind resides in its ability to thrive in the NOW, which is where all transformational power resides. Your choice of this book is an example of your use of the conscious mind to decide what to learn.

- The Subconscious Mind is impersonal and non-selective, and within it resides immense spiritual power, direction and creativity. It is at this level that we are connected to the Universal Law. The subconscious mind does not discriminate and does not choose; it only accepts what it receives from the conscious mind through repetition and emotion. Our subjective beliefs are a result of all the conscious thoughts we have passed to our subconscious mind through repetition. The fact that we can remember faces, names, passwords, and song lyrics are examples of thoughts that have taken root in the subconscious mind through repetition. A thought that has been combined with emotion will become a powerful habit that will help us or hurt us depending upon the nature of the thought. Your subconscious mind, once it has been imprinted by your conscious mind, will account for about 95% of everything you do and everything you attract into your life. So, as you learn to use your conscious mind in a way that consistently feeds your subconscious mind positive thoughts and feelings, you will have created a bridge to close the gap between your desires and a new, prosperous reality.

Unfortunately, millions of people unknowingly use the power of their thoughts for negative purposes, and much of the time they are not aware that a simple shift in consciousness can make a profound difference in their lives. These people go through life as powerless victims and accept life on the basis of what has happened in the past when they could have experienced this new, prosperous reality by making a shift in their focus and expectations. Are you ready to take advantage of the life-changing power of the mind to attract the money and prosperity you deserve? Millions of people are content with their boring lives and are unwilling to change, but what about you? Now that you know about the awesome potential within your mind you can no longer stand on the sidelines and just allow life to unfold with no positive direction or purpose. The power of your thoughts is creative energy in its finest and most dynamic form, and within the following chapters you will learn how to use this power to get whatever you want out of life. Are you up for the challenge?

CHAPTER 2

THE PROSPERING POWER OF AFFIRMATIONS

Affirmations are spoken statements of truth whose use goes back many centuries. Recorded history is filled with accounts of affirmations being used in mysticism, spirituality and religion. Some of the oldest forms of affirmative prayers go back to the ancient Egyptian culture in which hieroglyphs affirmed the majesty of mythical gods. In modern times, Catholics still recite rosary prayers in which affirmative statements are repeated in honor of the Virgin Mary. In Voodoo, which is an African-American folk spirituality, there is evidence of affirmative statements, as well. And New Thought spirituality, which developed during the late 1800s, ushered in the popular use of affirmations for those in the English speaking nations of the world. All these faiths, and in many others throughout the world, contain evidence of the use of spoken affirmations for spiritual well-being and physical health.

In the late Nineteenth Century Dr. Émile Coué popularized therapeutic affirmations such as "Every day, in every way, I'm getting better and better" through his personal method of psychotherapy and self-improvement. He wrote a popular book titled HOW TO PRACTICE SUGGESTION AND AUTOSUGGESTION, which was based on the idea of using affirmative statements for self-improvement. Decades later, Stuart Wilde and Louise Hay wrote AFFIRMATIONS and YOU CAN HEAL YOUR LIFE, respectively, in which readers were taught how to expand their personal power and heal their bodies and minds through the use of affirmations. These books were very effective and sold millions of copies, yet some readers got the impression that the repetition of words has a mystical power that can be used to make the Law of Attraction work. The truth is that the power to change our lives is not found in the words we speak because there is no creative power in words.

The power of affirmations lies in the way your affirmations make you FEEL, not in the words themselves. Your words, by themselves, have no power because they are merely the result of wind passing through your vocal chords resulting in sounds that are formed by your tongue. On the other hand, the feelings you experience while repeating affirmations is where the true creative power lies. All intentional creation is based on this feeling principle. Our feelings have the power to enhance our lives or to destroy them. For example, a person who feels unworthy of good things usually gets what is expected while a person who feels worthy of good things receives a mirrored response from the Law of Attraction. How we feel about money has a lot to do with how much money comes to us and what happens to that money. A person who feels that money is limited usually has little or no money by the end of the week because these feelings create circumstances that reflect what is felt inwardly. Dr. Maxwell Maltz wrote an excellent book titled PSYCHO CYBERNETICS in which he discussed the role that self-image plays in our individual worlds. He noted that a person will attract success or failure based upon his or her feelings of self-worth. The same holds true for the Law of Attraction, which responds to our predominant thoughts and feelings. So, what thoughts and feelings are you emitting as you read this sentence? Are your thoughts positive, uplifting and expectant? If so, your life should be one in which positive experiences are the norm. If not, then you can change that reality by taking an inventory of your beliefs and then reconstructing your thoughts and feelings through the information in this book.

Now that we understand the creative nature of affirmations, we can begin to change our lives through its power, but we must start slowly and then gain speed and intensity as we learn about the power of the Universal Law and how it responds to thoughts and feelings. The more we understand how this power works, the better will be our manifestations of wealth, health, or anything else we wish to experience through this creative power.

Neville Goddard, Dr. Joseph Murphy, and other spiritual visionaries explained that we must maintain the feeling of the wish fulfilled in order to attract our desires. In order to do this your creative affirmations MUST make you feel good and expectant. Your prosperity affirmations will not be effective if there is a negative feeling attached to them because the Law of Attraction will manifest the experience that matches the dominant feelings in your mind. Negative feelings are often based on fear or feelings of unworthiness. These beliefs often come from childhood and are established throughout life's challenges. If a person grew up in a household in which financial struggles were the norm, then that person might subconsciously expect to struggle throughout life. We have heard this theme over and over in statements such as "Nothing good ever happens to me" and "I can never get ahead in life!" All these negative statements attract negative experiences because they are firmly established beliefs within the minds of the strugglers.

    You cannot expect to manifest prosperity if you affirm "I am rich and prosperous" while not feeling rich and prosperous. If you do so you will only frustrate yourself, give up and will never manifest your desires. So, it is important to create affirmations that feel comfortable as you speak them. For example, a person who wants to attract a perfect mate might experience feelings of doubt by affirming, "I now have the perfect boyfriend who is romantic and thoughtful all the time." These discouraging feelings may arise because a former lover may not have been romantic and thoughtful. As a result, negative memories, feelings and beliefs can sabotage affirmations. So, a more effective affirmation might be, "I am now in the process of attracting the perfect boyfriend who is loving, romantic and fun to be with. I am doing this through the creative power of the Law of Attraction." This affirmation can be more effective for someone who is just learning about the Law of Attraction and the power that affirmations play in creating circumstances. "I am in the process of attracting" is a much more effective affirmation because it suggests action in which the desired relationship is being created by the Law of Attraction right now. In addition, affirmations of this nature stir up feelings of expectancy, which are some of the most powerful and creative feelings you can experience while speaking affirmations.

Affirming your way to financial prosperity is done by first taking an inventory of your feelings about money and then deciding whether or not you feel deserving of having more money. If so, how much money do you feel that you deserve? If you begin to uncover feelings of resistance you can still reprogram your mind to experience feelings of wealth and abundance. The key here is to determine where you are emotionally so that you can design affirmations that will not conflict with your current feelings, but which will stir up feelings of hope and expectation when spoken. For example, saying "I am infinitely rich and abundant and prosperous now" might stir up feelings of resistance because you might not feel rich and abundant now, so making this statement might feel like a lie. A better affirmation, which can stir up feelings of hope and expectation, might be, "I am in the process of attracting financial prosperity through the Law of Attraction" or "I am in the process of attracting my perfect job and increased income through the Universal Law." An important key to remember is that affirmations must be stated in the present, not in the future tense. To state "I *will* become rich and prosperous" is to suggest that you are not rich and prosperous now, which defeats the point of doing affirmations. All affirmations must be stated in the present tense because now is where your point of power is.

Here are a few examples of prosperity affirmations that can be used to generate feelings of wealth and expectation:

- I like money and I enjoy having it. I am now in the process of attracting more money and opportunities through the Law of Attraction.
- Having money makes me feel good, and I am in the process of having more and more each day!
- Money is my birthright, and I enjoy the thought of having lots of money. I am now in the process of attracting more financial prosperity through the creative power of my words and feelings.

You can use the affirmations presented here, but do not think that using them is mandatory. You can and should create your own affirmations. In fact, the affirmations that you create are the most powerful statements to use because they originate from your thoughts and feelings. Keep in mind that your feelings will attract wealth, not your words, so choose your affirmations wisely and do them with feeling for best results. You might notice that the statement "I enjoy the thought of having lots of money" makes you feel good. The reason for this is that most of us enjoy the thought of having lots of money. So this statement is not only true, but it feels good to affirm it. It is these positive and expectant feelings of wealth that we strive for in repeating affirmations.

Some people affirm for prosperity on the way to work or during the afternoon, and others speak affirmations just before going to bed. There is no best time to repeat affirmations, but studies have shown that they are more effective when done first thing in the morning. The reason for this is that upon awakening the brain is running at about 12 wave cycles per second and is most receptive to new ideas during this state. This is why a song that is heard upon awakening has a way of remaining in your thoughts all day long. In the morning, our subconscious mind is most fertile and receptive to suggestions. As a result, it is very important to start the day on a positive note by filling it with affirmative statements. Hearing the morning news is not the best way to start the day because it is often filled with negative stories and tragedies. Someone using the Law of Attraction to manifest money should start the morning with positive affirmations. An example of this might be, "I am excited about what the Law of Attraction has in store for me today! I look forward to all the prosperity and blessings this day holds." By starting the day on a positive note we establish the spiritual foundation for a creative and expectant day.

How long and how often affirmations are repeated depends on the person affirming. Some people are comfortable with five to ten minutes of affirmations per day while others do it longer. The length of a session is not as important as the good feelings aroused while affirming. A person who feels good after ten minutes of affirmations will generate more creative power than a person who affirms for an hour without feeling good, so be sure to focus on the feelings your words arouse. It is this creative power of feelings that will make you an irresistible money magnet.

CHAPTER 3

CREATIVE VISUALIZATION, PART 1

"Man moves in a world that is nothing more or less than his consciousness objectified."

- Neville Goddard

Creative visualization is one of the most powerful tools you can use to attract the desires of your heart. Visualizing daily can turbo charge the manifestation process and help attract the things you want quickly, but it can also be challenging if not understood and used properly. Once creative visualization is thoroughly understood, it will become much easier to use and more enjoyable in the long run. In fact, if you learn to visualize as outlined in this book, you will look forward to daily sessions with enthusiasm and you will understand that good things will come to you faster as a reflection of your changing consciousness. For the most part, creative visualization is more than just sitting on the couch and imagining that a new Mercedes is parked in your driveway or that you have just won the Powerball. It is much more three-dimensional than that, and it includes the use of senses such as hearing, imagined touch and vivid mental imagery. In fact, the use of imagined hearing and touch will add a rich dimension to your creative visualization exercises that will make your daily ritual lots of fun. But before delving into the use of this powerful practice we will look at the history of creative visualization to gain a better understanding of its power and influence over the physical world.

For starters, creative visualization is a process whereby the creative faculty of the mind is used to imagine having or doing something. For example, a man might imagine winning a large lottery prize, getting a promotion at work, owning a dream car, having the perfect girlfriend, or taking the vacation of a lifetime.

He would imagine seeing, feeling and experiencing what he would experience if his dream were a reality. A woman might use creative visualization to imagine her ideal marriage. She might imagine holding hands with her husband while feeling this reality with her awakened senses. She might even imagine feeling the wedding ring on her finger and the happiness that would be hers if this were her reality. In a nutshell, this is how creative visualization is done. In this chapter you will learn how it can be a fun, exciting and valuable tool to use for the manifestation of any goal.

The use of creative visualization goes back centuries, and probably much longer than that. The ancient cultures of the world were well aware of the power of creative visualization because we see evidence of it in ancient teachings, writings and myths. The book of Proverbs in the Old Testament, for example, reveals the importance of having a personal vision for success. It explains that where there is no vision, the people perish. This is figurative language to describe the failure that is the result of not having well-defined personal and spiritual goals. It is often said that a person with no goals or vision in life gets what he plans for: nothing.

The Lost Gospel of Thomas, which was discovered in 1945 near Nag Hammadi, Egypt, contains passages that modern mystics believe are references to the Law of Attraction. Although these passages do not explain the mechanics of this power, they clearly point out that this creative force responds to the coupling of two factors: thought and feeling. Lost for centuries, mankind had no idea of its insights and quantum implications until the gospel was found and studied. In it we read that Jesus said, "If two make peace with each other in a single house, they will say to the mountain, 'Move from here!' and it will move." This symbolic language implies that miracles occur (i.e., the "mountain" of lack will dissolve) once our thoughts and feelings are in agreement with one another. Intentional creation requires that we must, through the power of vivid imagination, generate feelings of wealth and abundance BEFORE we can attract prosperity. This is the key to manifestation. Once we have done this, our desires are guaranteed to materialize because the Law of Attraction responds to our thoughts and feelings by giving us what we imagine just like the law of gravity operates when a pebble is released from our grasp. In fact, the Law of Attraction is working for you right now whether you know it or not, believe it or not, or like it or not, as Bob Proctor says. It is always working for you and giving you exactly what you emit in terms of thoughts, feelings and beliefs.

    The Gospel of Thomas is only one example of a spiritual text that contains instructions about believing prior to receiving. The New Testament also records Jesus Christ as saying (Mark 11:24, NIV), "Whatever you ask for in prayer, believe that you have received it, and it will be yours." This passage clearly implies that the prerequisite for manifestation is to believe that we have ALREADY received what we want. This passage is the key to getting the money, cars, opportunities, and whatever else you desire. It tells us that we can have our desires as long as we persist in the feeling of already owning them. Unfortunately, this part of the manifesting equation has been overlooked for centuries. We are encouraged to ask and pray, but not to carry out the final step in the manifesting equation, which is to visualize.

The three-part manifesting process of Mark 11:24 is as follows:

1) Asking implies that we know exactly what we want. We must know exactly what we want before we can manifest it, but we must be willing to allow the Law of Attraction to deliver this desire from whatever channel it allows. Our job is to know exactly what we want, not to dictate how it will manifest for us. That is the job of the Universal Law.

2) Praying is the spiritual method that connects us with God. This is the step in which we look within for our connection to the creative spirit of the universe. Buddha, Christ and other ancient and modern mystics have taught that the Kingdom of Heaven is within.

3) Finally, this passage instructs us to believe that we have already received what we want and it will be ours. Creative

visualization is used in this step because persistent and vivid imagination helps us feel the reality of our desires, which attracts what we desire.

For at least 2,000 years monks in the Himalayan monasteries have used visualization and the creative power of feelings to heal, create peace, and to sustain their way of life high in the mountains. In fact, at least one modern writer and lecturer named Gregg Braden has traveled to the most remote parts of the world to learn how monks use the power of thoughts and emotions to heal the sick and create ideal physical situations in life. By speaking to monks through a translator, Braden learned that the creative impulse of the universe responds to human feelings. In other words, the most effective prayer is not a prayer of words, but a prayer which has its basis in human emotions. The astounding revelation about this discovery is that these positive feelings can be generated intentionally through the use of creative visualization. This model of reality suggests that there is no separation between humans and the creative power of the universe. We are all connected at the deepest level of reality, which is why the great spiritual masters of the ages have claimed that all humans are sons of God, figuratively speaking. In a scientific sense, Planck, Heisenberg and Bohm (who published Quantum Theory in 1951) echoed the same idea when they suggested that we are all connected on a quantum level. This idea is not as far-fetched as one can imagine when we understand that everything in the universe was once very closely connected. In fact, scientists say that if the space between all matter in the universe (between every atom's nucleus and orbiting subatomic particles) were removed, the result would be an object the size of a small green pea. The consideration of this amazing fact helps us comprehend the quantum connectedness of everything in existence.

> "Nothing can take it from you but your failure to persist in imagining the ideal realized."
> – Neville Goddard

The habitual practice of creative visualization influences two aspects of our being. The first aspect is our brain, which is where our consciousness resides for as long as we are alive. The second aspect is located within the realm of quantum reality, or spirit. As we feel the reality of our desires using creative visualization, millions of neural pathways are created within the brain to reflect the new beliefs, ideas, and good feelings that are experienced in our thoughts. These pathways are electrical in nature, and are described in textbooks as Neuroplasticity. It's a big word that is used to describe a relatively simple process in which neurons in the brain forge new connections when presented with new information. In essence, Neuroplasticity simply refers to the brain wiring and rewiring itself as it learns new things and unlearns old things. A demonstration of Neuroplasticity occurs when a pianist learns a sonata or when a child learns to ride a bike. As we visualize for money, for example, the good feelings we experience create new neural pathways in our brain that make the experience more familiar and enjoyable each time we visualize. This is similar to creating a path in the woods; the more the path is walked through, the more visible and pronounced the path becomes. New circuits can be created in as little as a week, and by 21 days it becomes a habit according to Dr. Maxwell Maltz who wrote PSYCHO-CYBERNETICS. As time passes, these new neural pathways become so deeply entrenched in our brains that each successive visualization session is easier to do and more enjoyable because a familiar, good-feeling habit is formed. If you do it correctly over and over, you will be drawn to visualize daily because your brain knows that it's a fun and rewarding exercise.

The second aspect of our being that is influenced by creative visualization is our spirit, which is a part of the Universal Law. As we visualize and feel the reality of what we want, our spiritual vibration is altered to reflect the vibration frequency that matches our desire. In other words, we inwardly become what we want in order to attract it. This is what brings it to us. A person who wants to attract more friends will embody and vibrate feelings of camaraderie in order to attract friends. The same goes for people wanting to experience more prosperity. As we generate feelings of abundance and express this in the form of thoughts, words and actions, prosperity comes our way. Since the Law of Attraction mirrors what we think, feel and do, we must be aware of what we are feeling and thinking at all times. We cannot be positive and expectant one minute, then negative the next minute and expect the Law of Attraction to deliver our desire unaffected. The late mystic Stuart Wilde said it best when he explained that the Law of Attraction reacts spastically to uncertain messages, so we must know exactly what we want and commit ourselves to vibrating these feelings to the Universal Law in order to attract our desires. Half-hearted commitment will produce a half-hearted response, so we must walk the path of commitment if we want this creative power to work for us. Creative mind can only give us what we are willing to accept, so we must keep this in mind as we visualize and expand our consciousness to achieve our goals. As we visualize regularly, we expand our beliefs to accept more, which brings us what we desire. Oliver Wendell Holmes said it best when he stated, "A mind that is stretched by a new experience can never go back to its old dimensions."

Modern mystics have written about the creative power of thoughts and how they can be used to attract what we desire. Some of the more notable books on the subject include Dr. Joseph Murphy's THE POWER OF YOUR SUBCONSCIOUS MIND, Dr. Ernest Holmes' THE SCIENCE OF MIND and YOUR INVISIBLE POWER by Genevieve Behrend. These teachers explained that we can change our life by changing our thoughts, but the most notable visionary who explained the art of creative visualization was Neville Goddard. He wrote many books and taught almost exclusively about the power of creative imagination. For over four decades until his death in 1972, Neville reached millions of people around the world through his books, recordings, and during personal lectures on stage, on television and through radio. His numerous books include FEELING IS THE SECRET, THE LAW AND THE PROMISE, and YOUR FAITH IS YOUR FORTUNE. His basic philosophy was that mankind, through the controlled use of imagination, can alter reality and make it conform to the dictates of thoughts. He believed in the supreme power of imagination and its ability to attract what is felt as real in the present. This is what he referred to as assuming the feeling of the wish fulfilled, thereby making outer circumstances conform to what is visualized and felt as reality.

Neville's teachings were backed up by a multitude of success stories. Among the many demonstrations of this power were overseas vacations he took as a young man even though he was broke at the time. He was later honorably discharged from the US Army during World War II after visualizing and feeling the reality of his freedom by imagining himself resting comfortably in his apartment. Soon thereafter he started a successful business, and then wrote many popular books and lectured in venues throughout New York City, Los Angeles, and San Francisco. Throughout his books he detailed the many successes of his students, and he demonstrated how anyone, through the proper use of creative imagination, could triumph over obstacles by using the power of thoughts and feelings. Among his students were successful businessmen, professional baseball players, television actors, singers, writers, doctors, and others who experienced immense success through his methods. Although he has been gone for decades, Neville's fame has extended well beyond the grave. Many contemporary books, radio, movie and television shows have referred to his teachings. Rhonda Byrne mentioned Neville Goddard in her best-selling book THE SECRET, and other best-selling authors have given him equal honor, such as Bob Proctor and Joe Vitale.

Jim Carrey, the famous comedian and actor, used the power of visualization to succeed in the movie industry. When he was out of work and unknown he used his thoughts, words and emotions in a creative way to become a rich and popular movie star. Knowing exactly what he wanted in life, he wrote himself a check for $10,000,000.00 on which he wrote "for acting services rendered". As he looked at the check every day, he imagined how he would feel to have ten million dollars in the bank, and he imagined himself making lots of successful movies. Of course, during this time he also kept busy perfecting his act and going on auditions. In addition to imagining himself rich and successful, he regularly drove up to the Hollywood Hills to look over the city while imagining the feelings of success. He has been quoted as saying that he would stretch out his arms over the evening panorama and say, "Everybody wants to work with me. I'm a really good actor. I have all kinds of movie offers." By doing this, Carrey employed the power of intentional creation to create his prosperous reality. A few years later he earned ten million dollars for starring in DUMB and DUMBER and has since earned many tens of millions of dollars appearing in successful movies. This legacy is a great testament to the power of creative visualization, but it does not end there. John Assaraf, best-selling author of THE ANSWER, THE COMPLETE VISION BOARD KIT and HAVING IT ALL, enjoys telling the famous story about how he bought the house of his dreams. Years before buying his dream house, he cut out a picture of the home (from a real estate magazine) and pasted it on his vision board. Looking at the image, he regularly and vividly imagined living there. In time, he actually bought that exact house but failed to make the connection between his new home and the picture on his vision board until later. The picture on his vision board was a scene from the back yard of his dream home, so it was easy not to recognize his new home in the image until a later inspection of his vision board revealed this surprising fact. He excitedly recalls how precisely the Law of Attraction had manifested his dream home. During speeches and interviews, he enjoys telling people that he did not get a home similar to the home on his vision board, but that he got the EXACT house he visualized through the Law of Attraction!

One of the most notable stories about attracting money through creative visualization centers around a lady named Cynthia Stafford who won $112,000,000.00 on a multi-state lottery game called Mega Millions. On the Ricki Lake show, she recalled the story about how she meditated on attracting money and imagined herself having a large amount of money. As she centered on thoughts of abundance, she felt the reality of her prosperity, which is how she communicated her desire to the Universal Law. On national TV that afternoon Cynthia told Ricky Lake that she willed her win through the creative power of her mind. She also mentioned that the Universe picked her winning numbers and delivered to her one of the largest lottery jackpots in history. You can find her story on YouTube.

CHAPTER 4

CREATIVE VISUALIZATION, PART 2

Now we will examine the four essential elements of creative visualization and how they can be used during your daily visualization exercises. These four elements, when used in harmony with one another, will help you to assume the feeling of the wish fulfilled thereby speeding up the manifestation process. The four elements are as follows:

- IMAGINED SEEING
- IMAGINED FEELING
- IMAGINED HEARING
- IMAGINED TOUCH

IMAGINED SEEING implies that we mentally see our goals as an imagined fact. This aspect of visualization utilizes the memory as it calls to mind images, pictures and scenes that reflect what we want to experience in life. For example, if you want to manifest a new Cadillac you will call to mind images of this car that are based on what you have encountered in real life, in print and on television. You might imagine seeing this car parked in your garage or imagine admiring a particular aspect of this car, such as the side view of the vehicle. Some people who visualize for a Rolls Royce focus on the look and details of the unmistakable Flying Lady grille ornament. The important thing is to know exactly what you want and how it looks from all angles, inside and out, whether you want money, a car, home, vacation, job, a relationship, or anything you can imagine experiencing.

IMAGINED FEELING refers to the emotions experienced during visualization. This is the most important aspect of the four elements. Neville Goddard told us to persist in the feeling of the wish fulfilled in order to manifest our desires, and the Gospel of Mark tells us to believe as though we have ALREADY received what we want. A belief is thought that has feeling behind it, such as a religious conviction, so we must add vivid feelings to our visualizations if we want to manifest our desires. For example, if your goal is to have more money and prosperity you must feel the feelings you would experience if your desire was a fact. Imagine how you would feel to have lots of money in the bank or in your possession. Imagine the happiness and excitement you would feel to have the car of your dreams, the love of your life, or your dream job. Radiate the feelings you would experience if your dream were a reality, and add to this excitement by imagining the money in your bank account or by mentally seeing the bank teller handing you a slip of paper reflecting a considerable account balance. By doing this you are adding IMAGINED SEEING to your exercise, which makes your exercise more powerful.

IMAGINED HEARING refers to the dialogue we imagine hearing and speaking during these exercises. This aspect of visualization can add a rich tone of reality to each session because some people, such as musicians, are more receptive to hearing than seeing. Certain words have a deep emotional impact for some people, such as "good", "great" and "fantastic", and these words can be used to enrich and deepen the visualization experience. The important point is to use positive imagined dialogue during each session to create the feeling of the wish fulfilled. For example, a man wanting a new job might imagine talking to friends about his new position. He might imagine hearing them make congratulatory statements about the job and he might respond by telling them about the wonderful perks of his new position. He might have a lengthy imagined conversation about how the job is perfect, how the salary is generous, and how much he loves the new opportunity. As he imagines this lively conversation, he would mentally imagine his new office while feeling the excitement of sitting at his new desk, thereby incorporating the first two aspects of visualization (IMAGINED SEEING AND IMAGINED FEELING) into this scene. As we layer imagined sensations and tones of reality to our visualization exercises, we are better equipped to manifest what we want because the emotion experienced is the catalyst that brings our dreams into reality.

IMAGINED TOUCH suggests that we mentally touch what we want to manifest. A person wanting more money, a new car, a vacation, or a new lover should use imagined touch to add a rich dimension of reality to creative visualization. A woman wanting a new lover, for example, might imagine feeling that person's face, arms, or kissing that person's lips. In terms of manifesting a new car, a man might imagine the feeling of sitting in his new car and vividly imagine how comfortable the seats feel on his back. The same goes for manifesting money. Vividly imagine what a tightly bundled stack of $100 bills would feel like in your hands. It takes one hundred $100 bills to equal $10,000.00, so feel the weight of that stack in your hands and feel the edges of the bills as you imagine your fingers holding the money. Use your memory to recall the scent of money, thereby adding another dimension of reality to this exercise. The more dimensions of reality you can add to this exercise the faster you will materialize your desires. As you imagine touching the money, vividly imagine the voice of a friend as she complements your prosperity. As you do this, imagine the intense feelings of financial prosperity and abundance that are yours as you see the money in your hands. By combining IMAGINED SEEING, IMAGINED FEELING AND IMAGINED HEARING to your IMAGINED TOUCH exercise, you become an irresistible magnet for what you desire.

Now that you have a better idea about how to make creative visualization work for you, you should begin visualizing each day for five minutes for at least a month. Once you have followed the advice of feeling good during these daily exercises, you will begin to establish an enjoyable habit. The important point to remember is that you must be persistent in your efforts because it takes at least 21 days to establish a habit. In addition, it would be unwise to begin by visualizing for more than five minutes per day. Once the habit has been established, you can increase it to fifteen minutes per day. The key here is persistence. You should be committed to visualizing daily even when you don't feel like doing it. This is why it is important to start with baby steps instead of committing yourself to an hour of visualization per day. You will have better results visualizing for five minutes per day than once a week for an hour. Neuroplasticity is best established within the brain when something is done regularly. Once you get into the habit of creative visualization and once it has been established in your brain, you will enjoy doing it all the time and will have better results with it.

CHAPTER 5

GRATITUDE AND RECEIVING

"The Universe Loves Gratitude."

- Louise Hay

As you develop a prosperity consciousness you should incorporate two powerful habits into your daily routine, the Practice of Gratitude and the Practice of Receiving. Metaphysically, they are powerful forces that can turn the tide of events for anyone on the road to a more prosperous future. You can use these tools to increase your financial prosperity, but they must be used daily to work effectively. Committing to daily spiritual work is similar to visiting the gym to build muscles: you cannot expect to build muscles by going to the gym once a week. Only daily commitment will result in the prosperous reality you desire.

Since the beginning of recorded history spiritual teachers have taught about the dynamic power of gratitude. They have explained that in order to get more of the things we want, we must emit feelings of gratitude for what we already have. Since the Law of Attraction creates events and circumstances to match our positive and negative feelings, we must take responsibility for the feelings we express throughout the day. If we feel good about life we will attract more things to feel good about, but if we feel bad about life and express negative thoughts and feelings throughout the day, we emit a vibration that attracts more things to feel bad about. This is why negative thinkers often compound miseries as their thoughts attract one negative event after another. Nikola Tesla, one of the greatest minds of the Twentieth Century, is quoted as saying, "If you want to find the secrets of the universe, think in terms of energy, frequency and vibration." It was his way of explaining that this triad is responsible for all that we experience in life. If you want a better idea about what your vibration is sending out, you should take an inventory of the events and circumstances of your life because they are an exact match to your vibration. The good thing is that you can change your vibration by changing your thoughts and feelings.

"It is impossible to bring more joy into your life if you are feeling ungrateful about what you have. Why? Because the thoughts and feelings you emit as you feel ungrateful are all negative emotions."

– Rhonda Byrne, author of The Secret

The act of gratitude is one of the most profound spiritual ideas to comprehend. It has such an immense effect in the spiritual world that if you learn one lesson from this book, it should be the importance of daily gratitude. The German theologian, philosopher and mystic known as Meister Eckhart, said that if the only prayer you ever say in your entire life is thank you, it will be enough. Although he lived many centuries ago, his words reflect the spiritual truth revealed in modern times through the study of quantum physics. Gratitude, because it is centered in feelings, profoundly impacts what happens to us on a daily basis. As we count our blessings and express grateful feelings for what we have, even if what we have is very little, we broadcast positive feelings into the Universal Law, which responds by giving us more to be thankful for. We can be thankful for the cool autumn breeze, clean drinking water, friends, our current job, or for the books we own or have access to at the library. We can be thankful for daily Internet access or for the penny we find on the sidewalk. We can even be thankful for memories of things that have happened to us, for our family members, or for our pets that make us feel good. There is no limit to the things to be grateful for. The point is to be thankful for something. Rhonda Byrne, in the Secret Daily Teachings, encourages readers to be thankful for their favorite music and for movies that encourage good feelings, for the telephone used to call friends, and even for electricity. She also encourages people to be thankful for their imaginations. Her uplifting words demonstrate that there is no limit to what we can be thankful for.

As we get into the spirit of daily gratitude, we will notice that this powerful practice accomplishes a number of things for us on a physical level and on a spiritual level:

- Feelings of gratitude encourage us to feel happy. These happy feelings release powerful chemicals in the brain that positively influence our mental state. The regular practice of gratitude will help us feel happy more often, which puts us in a mental state that is conducive to using the Law of Attraction.
- Positive feelings of gratitude change our overall spiritual vibration, which is the transformation needed to make the Universal Law respond to our vibration.
- As we raise our vibration from lack to abundance through the practice of gratitude, we will experience more wonderful things to be thankful for. As we persist in this new mentality we will reprogram our subconscious minds to the point where these new feelings will be natural and easy to maintain.

Sometimes being grateful for what we have is a challenge. Taking inventory of all the things we don't have or envying what people on TV own might have a discouraging influence over us. The trick is to stop focusing on what other people own. You don't know the intricate details of their spiritual path in life, so you should not compare your life to theirs. They might have a completely different spiritual evolution than you, and their possessions might be an integral part of their lesson in life. The most creative move you can make at this point is to turn your attention from the lives of other people and then focus attention on your life and your ability to manifest through the creative power of thought.

As you implement the practice of gratitude, you should start feeling grateful for the money that is on the way to you. Expectancy is a powerful force, which the writer of this book has used to win lottery prizes. As you emit feelings of gratitude for the money you desire, you will find yourself in a position to attract more money because these grateful feelings will attract circumstances to match your vibration. Keep in mind that abundance comes in all shapes and forms. It can and will come to you in the form of money, but it can also come in the form of free theater tickets, free vacations, dinners, clothing, invitations, and in other wonderful ways. There is no limit to the avenues of expression through which prosperity can manifest, so be open to receiving your desires from any channel that the Universal Law sees fit for expression. The fifty thousand dollars you desire, for example, might come from the lottery or it might come from an unexpected channel that you cannot possibly imagine, so always leave the details to the Universal Law. If you raise your vibration, the money will come.

Expressing gratitude does not require a lot of time or effort, which makes it an easy tool to use regularly. Gratitude can be expressed while alone or in the midst of people within the solitary confines of your thoughts. You can think of all the things you are thankful for as you cook dinner, wash dishes, walk your pet, or take a shower. You can speak affirmations of gratitude while driving to work or you can think about all the things you are grateful for as you ride the bus to school. A lady from Los Angeles uses her commute time to speak affirmations of gratitude as she travels the busy Los Angeles freeways. Her job is 22 miles away, so during the morning leg of her journey she speaks affirmations of gratitude while driving. A man in Boston keeps a gratitude journal in which he lists 20 things he is thankful for each day, and a man in NYC practices gratitude mentally as he jogs every evening through the West Village and then back to his apartment in Chelsea. There was even a video posted on YouTube in which a man discussed how he practiced gratitude while hiking up mountains. In San Francisco lives a lady who practices gratitude as she walks around her apartment and gives thanks for all she owns, such as her furniture, her comfortable bed, the food in her refrigerator, and even for the friends who visit her daily. The key is to practice gratitude regularly in order to consistently emit positive feelings. These grateful feelings are among the most powerful of all forces in the universe because they encourage you to focus on what you currently have and to feel good about them. And we all know, by now, that feelings are creative.

The following are some creative ideas to help you implement the practice of gratitude:

- Speak words of gratitude for at least five minutes per day. Once you have become accustomed to this habit then increase it to ten minutes per day. The key is to speak words of gratitude mindfully and with feeling.
- Daily, write down twenty things you are thankful for. You can start by being thankful for the Law of Attraction and for the fact that you have another day of life.
- Keep a gratitude journal that you can use throughout the day to record the things you are thankful for.
- Don't make excuses about not having time to practice gratitude. You can even practice gratitude while in the shower or while taking a bath. Think of all the time wasted on watching TV or surfing the Internet, and use some of that time in the practice of gratitude.

THE PRACTICE OF RECEIVING

The practice of receiving is one of the most powerful tools you can use to attract prosperity. Unfortunately, this practice is rarely mentioned in books and articles about the Law of Attraction. In fact, this might be the first time you read about this wonderful tool.

As we develop a prosperity consciousness we must pay close attention to our ability to receive whatever comes our way in terms of a cup of coffee, gifts, money, or anything that is offered to us. The Universal Law responds to all our thoughts, feelings, and actions. As a result, if we pass up things that are given to us (no matter how small or large) we are sending a strong message to the Universal Law about our ability and willingness to receive. By refusing what is offered to us, we are blocking the flow of prosperity that can transform our lives. Everything in the universe is energy, and by picking up that nickel on the sidewalk or saying yes when a coworker offers to buy lunch we are affirming that we are open to receiving all that comes our way. Do not take the practice of receiving lightly because it is a tremendously powerful tool that will help you attract money. The Universal Law does not distinguish between a penny and a million dollars because it can just as easily give either. So, as a daily exercise you should pick up all the pennies you find on the sidewalk and you should accept everything that comes your way even if you don't need what is offered to you. This means that you must say yes when a coworker offers to buy lunch or when someone is giving away free samples at the supermarket. The key here is to become comfortable with receiving and to start the flow of abundance through this daily practice.

By practicing receiving you will notice that the Universal Law will send more your way. You will get better parking spaces, free meals, gifts, books, money, and you might even win a contest or two! A lady in Los Angeles who learned about the practice of receiving entered contests and won a number of vacations, a new car, and cash prizes. As she opened her mind to receive more of what came her way, she eventually met the man of her dreams and got married to him. He owned a real estate brokerage, and gave her the prosperous life that her imagination created.

Even if you don't need what is offered to you, you can always give it away or throw it out. The key here is to learn to receive so that your actions become affirmations to the Universal Law that you are open and willing to receive. As you do this, miracles start to happen.

CHAPTER 6

LIVING IN BALANCE

"The Universal Law will never work for you until it can work through you."

– Eddie Coronado

In order to use the Universal Law we must understand that this power will only work through us, not for us. Since the nature of the Universal Law is characterized by order and harmony, our inner and outer actions must reflect its characteristics for it to respond to us. Another way of saying this is that in order to benefit from this power we must act and live in harmony with the nature of the Universal Law. I will explain more about this a little later. For now, let's look at the characteristics of the Universal Law to become familiar with this power:

- THE UNIVERSAL LAW IS IMPARTIAL: This means that you have as much access to this power as any other person on earth. You don't have to be particularly smart, the best looking, or a child of royalty to use this mighty force. We all have equal access to this power, and our effective use of it depends upon our ability to align to its nature.

- THE UNIVERSAL LAW IS UNEMOTIONAL: This power does not express anger or happiness or any of the emotions that we are accustomed to. It accepts us and loves us because we are a part of it. In addition, the Universal Law does not have an opinion about what you should experience in life. Similar to the way electricity is used to warm a house or to electrocute a person, this power simply responds to your thoughts, feelings and beliefs and reflects them back to you unemotionally in the form of everyday experiences.

- THE UNIVERSAL LAW IS NON-JUDGMENTAL: This means that the Universal Law accepts everyone without judgment about past or present circumstances. We are a part of its divine essence so it cannot judge or condemn us. It accepts us and allows us the time and opportunity to evolve, no matter how long this spiritual growth takes.

- THE NATURE OF THE UNIVERSAL LAW IS TO RESPOND TO US: The Universal Law will give us anything that we can feel and accept as truth. Since its nature is to mirror our beliefs, we must be very cautious about the thoughts and feelings we emit on a daily basis. It responds to positive feelings and negative feelings with the same dedication and intensity, so we must remain watchful in terms of what we think. This is why I say that the Universal Law cannot refuse your requests. It is always ready and willing to create events and circumstances based upon the quality of what you put into it.

Similar to the way in which water flows through a pipe, the Universal Law must move through your consciousness to manifest your desires. If your thoughts, feelings and actions are not in harmony with the nature of this power, you cannot expect it to work effectively. The power of the Universal Law is divine, and God cannot thrive in a soul that is filled with anything that is unlike itself. We move out of balance when we affirm prosperity in the morning but resort to negative thoughts and feelings in the evening, or when we affirm peace one minute and then start yelling at people the minute we get on the freeway. Since the universal law must work through your consciousness to manifest your desires, you must make the channel of your mind receptive and free of all inharmonious thoughts as much as possible.

The person who once engaged in negative thinking, criticism, and judgment against others must learn to uproot negative thoughts and then replace them with those that are in harmony with the Universal Law. This doesn't necessarily mean that you should invite old foes to lunch or start feeling good about those who have hurt you, but you must stop thinking about them to the best of your ability. Replace those negative memories with more important, creative feelings about what is now important to you and why you purchased this book. A wise person once said that a negative mind will never give you a positive life, so you should always look within yourself to determine what negative thoughts and beliefs need to be uprooted and discarded. Only by perfecting your mind will you be able to manifest the desires of your heart through the Law of Attraction.

The following thoughts, feelings and actions will place you out of alignment with the Universal Law:

- Negative Thinking

- Condemning

- Criticizing

- Judging

- Gossip

- Bitterness

- Jealousy

- Hatred

- Rudeness

- Remembering Past Hurts and Replaying Them Internally

- Revengeful Thoughts, Feelings or Actions

- Comparison

- Arrogance

The following thoughts, feelings and actions will place you in alignment with the Universal Law:

- Constant Gratitude

- Positive Thoughts

- Thinking Good About Ourselves And Others

- Creative Visualization

- Affirmations Laced With Positive Feelings

- Doing Things For Others

- Thinking Good Of Others

- Receiving What Comes To Us With Gladness

- Prayer and Meditation

- Contemplation

- Reading Books About The Law of Attraction

- Appreciating Nature

- Complementing People

- Looking At your Goal List Daily

- Laughing

- Hugging

Although monitoring thoughts and feelings all the time is challenging at first, it becomes much easier with time and commitment. The trajectory of spiritual growth is large and widespread; any small, positive changes you make will benefit you greatly in the long run. Like a pebble on a pond, positive thoughts and emotions will have widespread effects within the Universal Law once your consciousness has been cleared of all the barriers of negative thinking. Sometimes all it takes is a small shift in consciousness to go from barely making it in life to financial prosperity and abundance. The Universal Law is more than willing to create whatever you put into it, so be willing to offer it a clean canvas on which to paint the desires of your heart.

CHAPTER 7

QUESTIONS AND ANSWERS ABOUT THE UNIVERSAL LAW

Questions are powerful tools because they can open new doors for us and fuel our hope in what is new and unfamiliar. The answer to a question can set us on an entirely new path of excitement, hope and adventure. Instead of remaining hopeless and stuck in the same old rut, we can ask questions that can offer us a glimpse of hope for a better existence. You found this book in response to a question, which was, "How can I attract more money through the Law of Attraction?" So I hope that through the following question and answer section your curiosity will be satisfied.

QUESTION: Can I really win the lottery through the Law of Attraction?

ANSWER: In THE TRICK TO MONEY IS HAVING SOME, metaphysical teacher Stuart Wilde told the story about a woman who used the Law of Attraction to win a lottery jackpot of over $2,000,000.00 in cash. In California, a man won a lottery prize of $250,000.00 after using the Law of Attraction for a few months. So, the answer is yes, the law of attraction can be used to win a lottery prize. A person's financial success or failure depends upon one factor: an unyielding dedication to the creative power of the universe. This power, which can be used to manifest money, romance, a new job or anything we wish to experience, awaits our recognition and use, but it must be used in a specific way in order to work. The language of the Universal Law is that of feelings. It will bring us anything that we can believe in and feel as true. Remembering your past experiences with money can reveal your subjective feelings about it and help you learn more about yourself.

How do you feel about money? How do you feel about prosperity? Do you feel that you deserve prosperity and more money in the bank or do you feel that you deserve small amounts of cash dished out incrementally? You might even feel that you deserve to have some money in your savings account, but your ability to attract more is limited because you feel unworthy of having more. If this is the case, then you must understand that your beliefs about money will attract it or repel it from you. By healing our beliefs and feelings about money we can set ourselves on the road to attracting more prosperity and all that we desire, but we must be intent on sorting through all the negative feelings we have about money, and then replacing them with new beliefs. The very fact that we are willing to take an honest assessment about our money mindset means that we can start replacing old, limiting ideas and feelings about money. Dr. Nathaniel Branden (a popular self-esteem author) wrote that we cannot leave a place that we have never been to, so we must be willing to face our current mental situation if we want to improve it. Prosperity books, CDs, lectures and inspirational quotes are constructive ways of learning about and dealing with limiting beliefs about money. Once we replace these limiting beliefs we will be on the road to attracting the financial abundance we desire. A bit of advice about winning the lottery through the Law of Attraction is that, although it is possible to win a lot of money through the creative power of thought, a person developing a prosperity consciousness should not demand that the Universal Law deliver the money through specific avenues of expression. This is a quick way to block prosperity. A person who is intent on manifesting a lot of money should be open to receiving the money from all avenues of expression. The Universal Law has its own way of making dreams come true, which is usually in a manner more wonderful and more creative than can be imagined. A person desiring prosperity, for example, should acknowledge that a lottery win would be nice while recognizing that a financial manifestation can come through any number of channels. One particular lottery winner did not limit the creative power of the Universal Law by insisting that he win a lottery prize. He was committed to his affirmations and creative visualization exercises, and he regularly affirmed, "It would be nice to win the lottery but I am open to receiving money from any number of avenues because I know that the Law of Attraction can deliver my desire from any place." Having said this, he manifested a big lottery jackpot in an amazing way: he found the ticket! And then he went on to win more lottery prizes. This story demonstrates that anyone can manifest money through the Law of Attraction, and sometimes the demonstration will come in the form of a lottery jackpot or from another unexpected source.

QUESTION: What is a Vision Board?

ANSWER: A Vision Board is also called a Treasure Map, Dream Board or a Vision Map. Its purpose is to display images of the things you want. These images can contain words, pictures or images of the things you want to manifest through the Law of Attraction. You can get these images by printing them, drawing them, or cutting them out of magazines. A friend of the author uses magazine pictures to display on her Vision Board but she occasionally takes photographs of the things she wants and posts these images on her board. The Vision Board is not a magical tool. It has no metaphysical powers or properties. It is used to help us focus on what we want to manifest. By keeping and maintaining a Vision Board we are better equipped to focus on what we want because we see the images every day on our board. Each day, as we look at images of what we desire, we increase our enthusiasm and positive feelings about our desires, thereby directing the Universal Law to manifest our wishes. As we continue to look at these images, the familiarity of the thing desired becomes more natural to us and thus becomes easier to materialize. Your Vision Board does not have to be very large, so 8x10 inches is a good size to begin with. It should be made of cardboard or a heavy duty stock that can be hung or placed against a wall for daily viewing. Some people use a corkboard Vision Board on which push pins are used to affix images. In addition, words of affirmation can be added to the board, such as "I am in the process of manifesting my desires" or "I am a rich child of the Universe." The key to making a Vision Board work is to view it daily. Also, there is a lot of information about Vision Boards on the Internet and there are some very good online versions that can be used for free. Search for them on Google.

QUESTION: How long will my manifestation take to materialize?

ANSWER: Manifestation depends upon your ability to determine exactly what you want by stating your desires to the Universal Law through your thoughts, feelings and actions, and then living in alignment to the nature of this creative force until your wish has materialized. You can use this power to manifest ten dollars or ten million dollars. The choice is yours because the Universal Law does not have an opinion about how much money you should have. The problem that many people experience is that they become obsessed with reading every book on the market and never actually do the mental and spiritual work necessary to manifest their desires. A daily ritual of affirmations, visualizations, and living in harmony to the Universal Law must be employed. This will be discussed further in the chapter that features the Prosperity Action Plan.

QUESTION: Does my Zodiac sign influence my ability to attract prosperity?

ANSWER: Your zodiac sign has absolutely no impact on your personality or your future. No matter what astrologers claim, the truth is that only you have the power to create your destiny. Creative authors, hungry for a buck, created colorful horoscope readings to sell their services and books, so these readings should not be considered as reliable information. The Zodiac was created thousands of years ago by primitive people, and the word Zodiac actually means "circle of animals" which it depicts throughout its circuitous shape. These animals and associated symbols reflect the various events that occur during specific times of the year. The fish of Pieces, for example, is recognized during February and March, which is a season of the year when there is a lot of rain in the Northern Hemisphere. Lots of rain means lots of puddles and rivers and lots of fish. During this particular time the ancients did not have much luck hunting because the weather was cold and the ground was wet, but they had a lot of fish to eat. In June when the summer begins, the Zodiac sign is a crab. The reason for the crab is that during the Summer Solstice of June 21st the sun reaches the highest point on the horizon, and then it begins its one degree descent each day thereafter until it reaches the lowest point on the horizon, which is the Winter Solstice of December 21st. This rise and descent of the sun on the horizon is represented by an animal that walks in one direction and then in another: the crab. During the month of August we recognize the sign of Leo, or the Lion, when the weather is hot and the sun is like a roaring lion. And it goes on and on. As a result, we can see that the signs of the Zodiac have absolutely nothing to do with your destiny. They are merely symbols created to represent seasonal changes. Like William Shakespeare said, "It is not in the stars to hold our destiny but in ourselves."

QUESTION: What If I have a difficult time replacing negative thoughts?

ANSWER: The best advice is to spend as much time as possible reading and learning about the Law of Attraction. There are a number of good books and CDs on the market, such as those written by Bob Proctor, Joe Vitale, Neville Goddard, and Louise Hay. In addition, spend quality time each day affirming your prosperity and using your imagination to visualize what you desire. We will manifest what we desire when we have believed it, accepted it, and are comfortable with it. As we visualize daily we become more comfortable with what we want, we start believing that it's possible, and we begin to see it showing up in our lives more often. Although reading and learning is uplifting and necessary, no amount of reading will make up for quality time spent in creative visualization. This exercise must be done daily. In addition, give yourself credit for any small changes that you see in your consciousness as you learn more about the Universal Law. Sometimes a big change is a result of a small shift in consciousness, so always give yourself credit for every positive change you experience. And never give up because the Universal Law loves persistence!

QUESTION: What other tools or exercises can help me feel prosperous?

ANSWER: Some people use subliminal CDs to change their subconscious beliefs. A subliminal CD is composed of two tracks. One track features a sound, like ocean waves, while the secondary track features positive, life-changing affirmations that are created to address a number of issues, such as weight loss, self-confidence, memory enhancement, and prosperity. As the ocean wave track is heard by the conscious mind, the secondary track (containing affirmations) is absorbed by the subconscious mind. As a result, constant exposure to subliminal messages can produce life-changing effects for the person using the CD. The author of this book has used the Prosperity and Abundance CD by Progressive Awareness, which is the most reputable subliminal company in the world. Owned and operated by Dr. Eldon Taylor, author of numerous books, these subliminal products have helped scores of people improve the quality of their lives through daily use. Although a married person might not have the luxury of using a subliminal CD during sleep hours (when the CD would be most effective), he or she can experience favorable results using the CD during waking hours. Progressive Awareness can be found on the Internet by visiting their website at Innertalk.com. In addition, another exercise that can help a person feel prosperous is to hang out at expensive places once in a while. Hang out in the lobby of an expensive hotel and order some coffee, or visit a Rolls Royce showroom and experience the feelings of opulence in that showroom so that you can become comfortable with these feelings. If you live near an expensive part of town, you should go there and drive around, hang out and have an espresso, and become accustomed to how you would feel by living in that opulence. A friend of the author wanted a Mercedes Benz for the longest time, so he visited local dealerships, asked questions, got free brochures, and admired the car of his dreams up close. As his creative feelings became part of the act, he eventually got his new Mercedes in the most miraculous way. Today he is the proud owner of not one Benz, but two. He proved to himself that feelings are creative.

QUESTION: How long should I affirm and visualize per day?

ANSWER: Since creating through the Universal Law is primarily a matter of generating positive and expectant feelings, we should affirm and visualize for as long as it takes us to feel good about our exercises. For some people ten minutes is sufficient, but for others a little longer is required. Beginners should stick to a few minutes per day until a habit is formed. By then, a longer period will be easy to accomplish. The effectiveness of affirmations and visualizations is not determined by how many statements we make or how many mental scenes we can run through our mind. It is determined by how we feel when we do the exercises. If you can feel good after ten minutes, then you are on the right track.

QUESTION: What if I don't feel like visualizing?

ANSWER: Sometimes you will not feel like visualizing because it's human nature to get lazy once in a while or to become sidetracked, but the best time to visualize is actually when you don't feel like doing it. By visualizing when you're not feeling it you are sending a strong message to the Universal Law that you are persistent and, at the same time, you are overcoming the resistance to perform your visualization exercises. Once you embrace the resistance and deal with it, the act of visualization will become a pleasurable experience that you will enjoy doing each day. The most important idea here is that you must do it daily even if it's a challenge at first. As you show up daily and experiment with visualization, you will eventually learn what works for you.

QUESTION: What if I believe that life should be a struggle?

ANSWER: If this is what you grew up to believe then you are not alone. Lots of successful people have grown up in family situations in which struggle and lack was the predominant theme. The truth is that abundance and prosperity is your birthright and you can break out of old, limiting patterns through the creative power of your thoughts. Limitation and struggle is often the springboard that propels us from "just existing" to thriving in life. The very fact that you found this book and have made it this far means that you have the drive and the commitment to manifest a prosperous destiny through the Law of Attraction. Oprah Winfrey, Leonardo DiCaprio, Demi Moore, Mark Wahlberg, Celine Dion and a host of other famous people started off poor, but their vision of a greater life encouraged them to manifest their dreams. Oprah Winfrey, who believes in the Law of Attraction, said this about the power of thoughts: "I know for sure that what we dwell on is who we become."

QUESTION: If I play the lottery should I buy one ticket or lots of them?

ANSWER: If you create a prosperity consciousness and maintain the energy, then you will not need to buy lots of tickets. Buy only one or two, stick with a budget, and play for fun. You don't need to buy lots of tickets to make the Universal Law work. Do what you need to do on a spiritual level by affirming and visualizing, and then leave the rest to the Law of Attraction.

QUESTION: What should I do after I make my desire clear to the Universal Law?

ANSWER: My best advice is not to just sit around and wait for things to happen. Knock on doors, make cold calls, do what you would normally do during the course of the day. Listen to your hunches and always stay busy. There is an old saying that goes, "When you pray, move your feet." This means that you should not drop out of life when working on manifesting your desires through the Law of Attraction. A person wanting a better job, for example, should not stay home and wait for prospective employers to knock on the door. That person should do the spiritual work required to manifest a new job and then remain busy by connecting with people, filling out applications, and gaining the job experience or education required to meet the new position. Rarely will the Law of Attraction meet your needs if you do absolutely nothing. Even a lottery winner needs to buy a ticket, so the key to making this power work is to prepare for the manifestation of your desires by remaining in the marketplace so that your desires can manifest in the easiest, most effortless manner possible. By preparing for your manifestation you are affirming what you desire through your actions and expectations, which encourages the Law of Attraction to respond.

QUESTION: You say that the Universal Law is impersonal and unemotional, which gives me the impression that it's an uncaring power?

ANSWER: The fact that the Universal Law is impersonal and unemotional does not mean that it is an uncaring power. We are a part of it and it is a part of us, so this impartiality is more like an unconditional love. It loves us so much that it will allow us all the time in the world to evolve, whether it takes a few weeks, a few years, or a few lifetimes. It gently encourages us and waits patiently for us to evolve to higher levels of existence. When we feel inspired to evolve spiritually, we can be sure that the Universal Law is doing the inspiring.

QUESTION: If I play the lottery should I pick my own numbers or let the machine pick my numbers?

ANSWER: If you provide the consciousness of wealth and abundance, then it does not matter if you let the machine pick your numbers or if you pick them yourself. The Universe will respond to your thoughts and feelings of wealth and deliver the money from any number of channels, including a possible lottery win. Work on your prosperity consciousness and be open to receiving the money from anywhere, and it will come. Guaranteed.

QUESTION: Am I guaranteed to prosper by using this power properly?

ANSWER: Yes, definitely! The Law of Attraction has no choice but to respond to your prolonged thoughts and feelings. It cannot and will never say no to you, so you might as well use it for your good. It will respond to you as long as you provide the consciousness of wealth and maintain those thoughts and feelings until your desires have materialized. This is the way I won the lottery twice, and it's the way that others have manifested prosperity. This power has never let anyone down. Give it a try, and persist until you have manifested your desires.

QUESTION: Do good luck charms, spells, candles and talismans work?

ANSWER: They work for people who believe in them because the expectation makes them work, but they are of no use to the person who has learned the true nature of the Universal Law. A person who has learned that she is a part of the God force only looks within for true personal power.

QUESTION: How can I learn to relax more while doing my visualization exercises?

ANSWER: One of the main problems beginners have is the inability to relax and concentrate during these exercises. In addition to having a quiet space in which to visualize, you might consider drinking green tea during your exercises. Green tea contains a powerful amino acid called theanine, which is known for its ability to relax the mind and body. Although it contains a small amount of caffeine, its calming effects far outweigh the effects of caffeine. When ingested, the theanine in green tea instantly starts to relax the body and mind, which helps promote relaxation during visualization exercises. The author of this book drinks Bigelow green tea with mint because it tastes good and provides a calming effect. Visualization sessions are easier to accomplish and more effective once intruding thoughts and anxieties have been pacified through the use of this drink.

QUESTION: What if I don't enjoy repeating affirmations?

ANSWER: If you don't enjoy repeating affirmations regularly then you should consider spending more time doing creative visualization exercises. You can actually incorporate affirmations into daily life by using your words wisely and being positive about everything you say. Our words have tremendous power, so use them wisely at all times. When faced with a scenario in which you have the power to describe a situation, use words that are creative and uplifting. For example, instead of saying something negative about a person or situation, you might affirm that you have no comment or that you would rather talk about positive things. You might even send that person or situation a verbal blessing, but never speak words of negativity when neutral or positive words will do. In addition, by their very nature, men are more inclined to visualize because they are wired in a way that responds to what is seen through the eyes or as a mental scene. Men can easily get excited about seeing cars or a homerun at a baseball game because of their internal wiring. Women, on the other hand, sometimes enjoy affirmations much more because of their internal wiring that is more receptive to words and the feelings associated with words. The point is to do more of what feels good to you. When you feel good, you create.

CHAPTER 8

THE PROSPERITY ACTION PLAN

Before presenting my Prosperity Action Plan there are a few things I want to cover. The first important point to consider is that change takes time. It might not take years to get what you want to manifest, but it might take a number of months depending upon the amount of negativity you need to work through in your mind. I manifested my first major prosperity demonstration within a few months of learning about the Law of Attraction. At that point, it took a few months of committed inner work to change my limited beliefs about money enough to manifest what I wanted. During this time I persisted in mental and spiritual work knowing that my efforts would produce success if I worked with the Universal Law and allowed it to flow through me, as discussed in the Living in Balance chapter. As my beliefs changed, money and other things began to show up in remarkable ways. I got a promotion at work, people started giving me money and inviting me places, and I won some wonderful lottery prizes. Twice I found a $100 bill on the street, which encouraged me to believe that this power was responding to my changing beliefs. It's important to understand that your prosperity might show up in small ways at first, but will increase in regularity and magnitude as you persist in working with the Law of Attraction. As you see positive changes happening around you, you should take the time to acknowledge these changes and feel grateful for the good that is on the way to you. How you react during this waiting period is very important because the Universal Law will respond to persistence OR frustration, depending upon what you emit in the form of thoughts and feelings. Feeling frustrated and impatient means that you are afraid that the Law of Attraction will not deliver your desire, and if you emit these feelings you will get more of what you are feeling. But if you commit to this plan and express feelings of expectation, you will encourage the Universal Law to deliver your desires.

A few ideas to keep in mind as you commit to the Prosperity Action Plan are as follows:

- You should always be aware of what you are thinking throughout the day. Sometimes this may be challenging, but it's a task that has rewards. Try to keep your thoughts focused on positivity and expectation at all times. This does not mean that you must take up the Pollyanna mentality, but you must monitor your thoughts by making sure that you are not expressing negative thoughts and feelings. Mental replays of arguments you had in the past, how you felt after someone hurt you, or critical thoughts and feelings that pop up from time to time will negatively affect your mental atmosphere, so you must always be aware that your current thoughts and feelings are telling the Universal Law what you want to experience more of.

- A single, undirected thought does not have much power, but through repetition your thoughts become highly concentrated and powerful. The more you focus on getting what you want through the Law of Attraction, the more powerful your thoughts become and the faster will you manifest what you want.

- One of the biggest mistakes people make when working with visualization is assuming that you only have to visualize once. This is not true. A weight-lifter doesn't build up muscles by visiting the gym once a year. He builds muscles by working out daily, which is why you should not miss a single day of this action plan. If, for some reason you must miss a day, then you should get back to it the following day and try not to miss another day of using this action plan.

- Never look for signs. Looking for them can encourage us to feel anxious. The power that you are working with is omnipotent and will respond to your commitment, so you should not spend your mental energy looking for signs. They will show up once you have created a mental equivalent of what you desire. A gardener who plants a seed does not dig up the seed to make sure that it is growing. He tends to his garden by watering it regularly. If you commit to this power your desires will manifest when you least expect, and will show up in amazing ways.

THE PROSPERITY ACTION PLAN

(THIS IS THE ACTION PLAN I USED TO MANIFEST MY LOTTERY WINS)

"Creation is always happening. Every time an individual has a thought, or a prolonged, chronic way of thinking, they're in the creation process. Something is going to manifest out of those thoughts."

– Michael Bernard Beckwith

Write down the things you desire. Do not allow your past experiences to influence your choices, but decide exactly what you want. The Universal Law, which is a part of you, can and will manifest the things you desire, so you must be clear about what you want. Revise your list for a day or two until you feel comfortable with it. A first draft is rarely perfect, so take some time and be sure that the finished list is a reflection of what you really want. There is no magic in writing your desires; this method allows you to see your desires on paper and provides a focus point that you can look at regularly, which is similar to the way a Vision Board is used.

- READ THIS LIST FOUR TIMES A DAY: upon awakening, during the middle of the day, just before dinner, and again before bed.

- THINK ABOUT WHAT YOU WANT THROUGHOUT THE DAY and understand that the Law of Attraction is responding to your thoughts and feelings. You always get more of what you think about.

- ALWAYS THINK ABOUT YOUR DESIRES AS THOUGH YOU ALREADY HAVE THEM. This is where Neville Goddard's advice comes in handy. By thinking about your desires as an accomplished fact, you are providing the mental state that will bring about the manifestation of your desires. Use visualization and affirmations throughout the day to feel good about what you are manifesting.

- BE OPEN TO RECEIVING WHAT YOU DESIRE FROM ANY CHANNEL that the Universal Law sees fit. If you want more money, you can get it from any number of avenues, but do not limit the Universal Law by demanding that the money show up from a specific channel, which will only block the flow of prosperity. Ten million U.S. dollars is still money whether it comes from the lottery or from another unexpected channel, so be open to receiving it from anywhere.

- DON'T TELL ANYONE WHAT YOU ARE DOING. You must keep your manifestation work a secret. Talking about your desire dissipates the spiritual energy you have built up. Once you manifest your desires you can share the Law of Attraction with all your friends, but secrecy is the key as you begin this journey. Critical friends and scoffing bystanders can sidetrack your efforts, so you must keep this spiritual work a secret unless you have a close friend who believes in the Universal Law and is on the same path.

- NEVER GIVE UP because your manifestation is guaranteed through the Law of Attraction. What you want belongs to you, but you must create it in consciousness first. When that has been done, your manifestation will be delivered.

Persistence is the key to making this action plan work, so be patient with yourself and stick to the plan. At the perfect time, you will manifest the desires of your heart and then you will understand how powerful and easily accessible the Law of Attraction really is. Also, keep in mind that no amount of reading will take the place of actually doing the exercises in this book. The infinite power of the Universal Law is set in motion through action because everything in the universe is energy, from the smallest subatomic particle to the largest star in our galaxy. Nothing is stagnant, and neither should you be. Your days should be characterized by constant learning and commitment to these principles. As you follow these suggestions you will arrive at the point where you will look back upon your life and wonder why it took you so long to make the decision to change your life by changing your thoughts. The entire Universe wants you to prosper, but it waits for you to realize this and claim what is yours.

If you enjoyed this book, please read my other books:

HOW TO WIN THE LOTTERY WITH THE LAW OF ATTRACTION: FOUR LOTTERY WINNERS SHARE THEIR MANIFESTATION TECHNIQUES

ADVANCED LAW OF ATTRACTION TECHNIQUES: MASTERING MANIFESTATION AND ATTRACTING WHAT YOU WANT FAST

THE POWER OF YOUR SPOKEN WORD: 300 POWERFUL AFFIRMATIONS FOR MANIFESTING MONEY AND MASSIVE SUCCESS

Eddie

Manufactured by Amazon.ca
Acheson, AB

12944254R00061